Harvest of Hope

There are two elements here—
truth and beauty;
beauty in the hearts of lovers,
and truth in the arms
of the tillers of the soil.

Kahlil Gibran

Harvest of Hope
SERRV International
Phil Grout

Library of Congress Control Number: 2003091587

ISBN: 0-9708816-2-2

SERRV International
122 State St. Ste.600
Madison, WI 53703
(608)255-0440
www.serrv.org

Other books by Phil Grout

A Spell in Plains
Seeds of Hope

To Afua

"I could not deny that old woman."

Emmanuel Opoku, Recorder
Odaho Society Kuapa Kokoo

I couldn't either.

Helena Bempong, cocoa farmer

Foreward

Pauline Tiffen co-founder Kuapa Kokoo

This beautiful book tells the tale of a special woman you will never meet—Helena Bempong, a cocoa farmer from Odaho, Ghana. Her story is important because she is one of more than three million cocoa farmers. They carefully and skillfully grow just a few sacks of cocoa beans each year, on their tiny farms in Africa and Latin America.

Helena is an expert, and her beans would pass the toughest quality test. Yet who recognizes this? It is not as if Helena and her fellow farmers are new in the business. Cocoa is an ancient trade. West Africans have been growing cocoa for many generations. The first "modern" chocolate bar was made back in 1847 by an English Quaker, Mr. Fry. As the decades have passed, large fortunes and billion-dollar companies have evolved, spanning the globe with their tempting confections.

But cocoa is an anonymous universe. Companies do not reveal or celebrate the lives of people like Helena without whom they could not ply their trade. And we chocolate lovers are part of this disconnect too. The gap is great between the pleasure of a fine chunk of chocolate melting in the mouth and the far away origins of this hand-picked and carefully tended crop .

Today, Helena and many in her village are proud members of a cooperative called Kuapa Kokoo, literally "Good Cocoa Farmer". But it was not always so. Farmers were at the mercy of unscrupulous officials who cheated them by fixing the weighing scales, confiscated their land and belongings, seldom paid for cocoa in full, or used checks that bounced and were always finding fault, even where there was none. Farmers had no voice, and no recourse to anybody. Some pioneering farmers were despairing at their treatment, their isolation and their lack of dignity. "We are not farmers," said one I interviewed in 1993, just before Kuapa Kokoo's formation. "We are just 'tree minders' for others who come and take what we have." But now, ten years later, the Kuapa Kokoo village network includes more than 40,000 farmers, each organized as a democratic group with a special place for women farmers like Helena. Their cooperative activities are spread out across more than 600 villages in all the main cocoa growing areas of Ghana.

It took much courage and effort to organize Kuapa Kokoo—quite against the odds and weight of history. To even start a farmer-owned cocoa trading company looked insurmountable. Seen as just illiterate peasants, they were presumed to be stupid. They needed only the chance to show they could borrow money and repay it; that they knew their trade; could guarantee fine cocoa as well as deliver it 100%. They also had to overcome the worst kind of obstacle—the disbelief and skepticism of others. Year by year, sack by sack, farmer by farmer, this cooperative network has transformed totally invisible producers at the end of an anonymous and unaccountable global trading supply chain into dignified members of a respected cooperative. The organization speaks out for them, profitably trades their cocoa, accounts for every cent from every member, and supports hundreds of community projects to improve access to water and education.

And in 1998 these farmers made a unique move to bridge the gap between cocoa farmer and chocolate consumer. They launched their own chocolate bar called Divine—a medium for telling their story far from their villages to chocolate lovers worlds away.

Emmanuel Opoku, Kuapa Kokoo recorder, Odaho Society

Helena and the other Kuapa Kokoo farmers like her across Ghana have welcomed Phil Grout—and through his thoughtful vista, us too—into their communities. Few who have journeyed into the lives of the Helena Bempongs of the world have the sight, the empathy and the heart of wanderer, Phil Grout, who is able to tell so much and make something so otherwise emotionally and physically distant, so close and important to us. This is an overture for us to play our part and overcome the gap between our worlds, while celebrating our irresistible connection through Divine chocolate. This book is an invitation. Come to a special world where chocolate matters.

Nwtafrn Gomygo pushes with his feet while his friend Augustine Onwath pulls with his hands to create a pretend truck from a discarded timber, broken bamboo pipes and their imaginations.

Preface

I hear my feathered friend cackling in the hibiscus tree just outside my sleeping place. He's happily drinking nectar from the scarlet blooms. They go nicely with his green shirt, black belly and red nape. Underneath the cackles I can hear the constant singing of cicadas, punctuated by an occasional bleat from a stray lamb looking for its mother who has probably found shade from this 100 degree heat. I've found shade on this bed, but not enough relief to carry me off to a good catnap.

Rivulets of sweat are starting to run in my ears when I hear a new sound outside. First it's hushed giggles followed by a hollow crunching sound—then more giggles. I roll off the mattress and pop my head up over the garden wall and find two boys sitting on a board. They haven't discovered me watching them. They're intent on their invention.

Now the board is moving—somewhat rolling, on two short lengths of bamboo pipe. The boys sit back-to-back on the board. One boy in sandals digs his heels into the dirt and pushes, while his friend uses his hands to pull. The energy of the pushing and pulling is transferred to the relative roundness of the bamboo "wheels", and the boys achieve a bit of locomotion. When one of the trailing bamboo "wheels" nears the end of the board, the boy in the rear pulls the bamboo out and hands it to his partner who inserts it under the front of the board. The boys use their imaginations to fashion a pretend truck out of a discarded wooden plank and two short lengths of bamboo, all propelled by two feet and two hands. Slowly they move across the dirt and gravel.

I'm struck with the fact these boys are using their creativity and determination to create a means of playful transportation from discarded, seemingly worthless objects—broken wood and bamboo. It may seem inconsequential, but through their own initiative, the boys have made their lives a little better. They are living in a tense which occurred to me the other day— the *perfect present.* I see people of all ages in this village living in the *perfect present,* with their simple lives moving gracefully as cocoa farmers through some of the toughest manual labor I've ever witnessed. There is a beauty to their lives which is connected to their reliance on the earth as farmers. Much of their toil is executed in the same way it was eons ago—with their hands, using tools quite similar to what existed in Neolithic cultures thousands of years ago. Fire, the wheel, toolmaking and agriculture all grew out of imaginations not so dissimilar from that of the boys living in the *perfect present*, motivated by the instincts of survival like those of a green and black bird with red nape drinking nectar from a hibiscus bloom.

These boys are the sons and grandsons of cocoa farmers who for generations have gone about their daily lives moving to the rhythms of the land and the cycles of cocoa. It's a rhythm felt throughout the Developing World of people living in concert with the earth and connected to each other by the earth. We in the more developed regions of the world have much to learn from these people who live a very basic existence, not in a perfect world, but in a world of the *perfect present* where life, with all of its harshness, is beautiful.

Phil Grout
Odaho, Ghana

Cocoa beans dry in the afternoon sun on a bamboo drying rack outside a typical cocoa farmer's home in Odaho, Ghana

Acknowledgements

SPECIAL THANKS TO MY FRIENDS IN ODAHO:

Helena Bempong who fed me food for body and soul
Paul Bempong who gave me friendship and translations
Emmanuel (Emma) Opoku who gave me friendship, insight and inspiration as well as Mary, Agnes, Josephine, Philamena, Peter, Afua, Paul, Samson, Badu, Kwame, Kofi, Patrick, Augustine, Mathew, Joyce, Frank, Veronica, Richard, Margaret, B.K. and many more. . .

Mark Gyan who gave me lodging in Odaho

Odaho Society Kuapa Kokoo Ltd.
Anthony Bempong, President
Emmanuel Opoku, Recorder

Kuapa Kokoo Ltd.
Pauline Tiffen, Co-Founder
Kwabena Tinyase-Ohemeng, Managing Director
Nickolas Adjei-Gyan, Manager Research and Development
Nuruddin Boateng, Research and Development Officer

SERRV International
Robert Chase, President
Serena Sato, Special Projects Coordinator
Sam Tokheim, Chocolate Coordinator
Dan Schaller, Information Systems Manager
Brian Backe, Development Director

Day Chocolate Co.
Jacqui MacDonald, Chairman of the Board
Sophi Tranchell, Managing Director

NOTES ON THE PRINTING

Designed by Phil Grout / the Studios@TreeHouse
2658 Patapsco Rd. Finksburg, Maryland 21048
philgrout.com
composed in 11-point Times New Roman with Mona Lisa and Times New Roman display
Printed on 80-pound Mead Sterling Dull by Wilmer Printing, Inc., Timonium, Maryland

NOTES ON THE PHOTOGRAPHS

All images are by the author, except where noted, and were digitally captured on an Olympus E-20N camera at SHQ 1/2.7 for approximately 3 mgb. files

Field imaging (Africa) done on an Apple i-Book laptop using Adobe Photoshop 7.0

Final imaging (Maryland) done on an Apple G-4 (433mghz) computer using Adobe Photoshop 7.0

BOOK DESIGNED in Quark XPress 4.1

CARTOGRAPHY: Special thanks to Beth N. Weisenborn who graciously offered her talents at the 11th hour

BOTANICAL CONSULTANTS: (Feather & Associates)
Drs. Maria Barbosa and Tolbert Feather

. . .AND AT HOME

Dad who sent a feather — Mother who sent light
Fred who gave me song and companionship with each word.

. . .ML, without whom. . .

Introduction

Cocoa comes from the plant *Theobroma cacao* ("food for the gods")—a tree which has been cultivated for thousands of years. Today more than 20 million people around the world depend on cocoa for their livelihood. About 90 per cent of cocoa production comes from small land holdings averaging about 12 acres. The cocoa tree evolved in the upper Amazon basin in Brazil and spread throughout Central America and into Mexico. South American "Indians" apparently sucked on the sweet mucilage covering the cocoa seeds and also fermented this pulp to make a beverage, but they discarded the seeds. Cocoa farmers of Ghana still take a break in their work to suck on the sweet, thick membrane; then spit out the seeds.

A mature pod from the tree, *Theobroma cacao*, contains 30 to 40 seeds which are dried into cocoa beans before becoming chocolate.

The Aztecs called the cocoa tree *cacvaqualhitl*, the beans *cachoatl* and a special drink they made from the beans, *chocolatl*. The cocoa beans were sun dried, roasted and ground on stone metates with the addition of water, vanilla and red annatto seeds to make a paste which would dry into cakes for storing. The cake would be placed in a gourd, water added and poured back and forth to make a blood-red frothy beverage (possibly the Pre-Columbian ancestor to the *latte,* and probably a lot cheaper).

In 16th Century Nicaragua, cocoa seeds were used as money. A rabbit could be purchased for 10 beans, a horse or mule for 50 and a slave could be bought for 100 cocoa beans. But the Spanish *conquistadores* became devotees of cocoa as a beverage. However, since the *chocolatl* was actually money, only the wealthy could afford to drink it. It's believed that Christopher Columbus was the first European to encounter the *chocolatl* drink, but its full appreciation wasn't realized until Hernando Cortes witnessed the Aztec king Montezuma being presented with 50 golden bowls of the exotic drink in 1519. Reportedly Cortes threw a party back in Spain 11 years later and served *chocolatl*, but his guests thought it was bitter. Sugar spread the popularity of cocoa throughout Europe in the 17th Century.

Chocolate houses were gaining prominence over the traditional coffee houses in 18th Century England. Then someone came up with the idea of adding brick dust to the brew to thicken it (*lattemachismo)*. That drink never made it out of the focus group. The Industrial Revolution in the early 19th Century, which speeded up cocoa processing, plus a drop in import duties on raw cocoa beans, made chocolate drinking affordable to the masses, not just the wealthy.

Conrad van Hooten, a Dutch chemist, discovered in 1828 that the fat in the roasted chips, or "nibs", of cocoa beans could be pressed out and separated. Cocoa powder was left, and the cocoa butter could be used for other purposes. Seventeen years later quite an important purpose for that cocoa butter was discovered by Dr. Joseph Fry. He mixed cocoa butter with some of the cocoa nibs and added sugar to create the first chocolate bar. In 1876 Daniel Peter invented the first milk chocolate, and 28 years later someone mixed chocolate with milk to make chocolate milk (without brick dust, of course).

While Europeans were experimenting with their chocolate and how to consume it in the 19th Century, agronomists in Latin America were improving the types of *Theobroma cacao.* At the same time, trade between Brazil and West Africa was on the rise, and slowly cocoa was also coming to fruition for the ancestors of Helena Bempong and her fellow Ghanaian farmers. It started with cocoa cultivation in 1822 on the tiny island of Principe, in the Gulf of Guinea near Gold Coast (now Ghana). Cocoa spread to the mainland through Cameroon and Nigeria, and then in 1879 the *amelonado* type of cocoa was introduced successfully in Ghana. Cocoa also flourished in neighboring Ivory Coast which eventually became the world's leading producer of cocoa. Ghana is second.

Dried cocoa beans are roasted, ground and the "nibs" of cocoa are added to cocoa butter, sugar and milk to make a Divine Chocolate bar.

The cocoa cultivated by the farmers of Odaho in this story was first planted in the 1920's by farmers moving from the western part of Ghana near Ivory Coast. The grandfather of Anthony Bempong, Helena's husband, was one of those cocoa pioneers. He and his brother built the family compound where the Bempongs live today, and the brothers also planted the cocoa land Anthony and Helena are still farming. Anthony's sister, Mary Kwayie, farms another portion of that same ancestral land.

Demand for cocoa is high outside the Developing World. The British Broadcasting Company recently extrapolated that Cadbury sells enough of its Dairy Milk chocolate bar in one year to cover 430 soccer fields. The International Cocoa Organization (ICCO) estimates the world-wide confectionery industry, including sugar and chocolate, generates approximately $80 billion annually in retail sales. The Chocolate Manufacturers Association calculates that the retail chocolate industry in the U.S. was $13 billion in 2000. The Swiss eat more chocolate than any other group of people in the world. They averaged 22.4 pounds of chocolate per person in 2000, followed by the British at 17.5 pounds. Americans were eleventh in chocolate consumption that year, averaging 11.6 pounds per person. This contrasts to the entire continent of Africa where all Africans consumed an average of 5.1 ounces of chocolate per capita for that same period. That's the equivalent of one medium-sized Divine Chocolate bar.

Of Cuckoos, Cocoa & Kok'oo

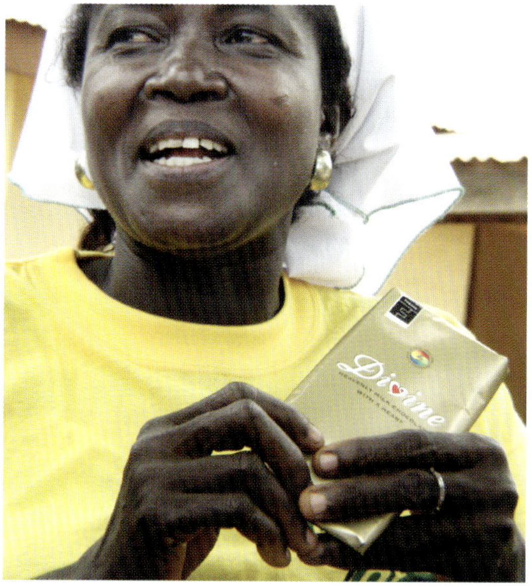

Cocoa farmer Helena Bempong gets ready to enjoy some of the fruits of her labor—a Divine chocolate bar.

This is the story of cocoa farmers in Ghana—particularly Helena Bempong—whose primary crop is the main ingredient in chocolate. It may seem like a long way from Helena's cocoa groves in West Africa to post World War II reconstruction in Germany, but some of that distance has been shortened by an organization called SERRV International. The roots of SERRV go back to relief efforts in rebuilding Europe in the wake of the destruction of the war. German refugees lacked just about everything except hope and to build on that hope various relief groups including the Church of the Brethren provided the means for the displaced to reconstruct their lives. The Brethren are traditional pacifists, grounded in peace and reconciliation. The Protestant denomination shipped herds of dairy cattle to Europe to provide an important food requirement to the survivors. While distributing the cattle throughout Germany, the "cowboys" as they were called, discovered that traditional, handcrafted cuckoo clocks had also survived the war. Clocks were purchased, brought back to the United States and sold to customers who appreciated the craftsmanship. Soon other handcraft items from Europe were added to the inventory, and what is now SERRV International—an independent non-profit alternative trading organization—was born.

Today SERRV draws from skills of artisans in every region of the world with the goal of assisting low income people and their organizations to develop the capacity, skills and resources to survive and succeed in the new global economy. SERRV connects handcraft artists with appreciative customers, and in the end, makes certain craftspersons are paid fairly for their skills, and customer are charged a fair price. It's about maintaining Fair Trade practices, ensuring safe working conditions, promoting social progress and preserving cultural concerns of all people.

As an outgrowth of their Fair Trade commitment, SERRV International has been selected by Day Chocolate Company (U.K.) to distribute Divine Chocolate in the U.S. Day's chocolate comes from cocoa grown by Helena and about 40,000 cocoa farmers like her in Ghana who are members of a new cooperative, Kuapa Kokoo ("good cocoa farmer"). The farmer members of Kuapa Kokoo are not only guaranteed a set price above the world market price for their cocoa, they also receive bonuses for their efforts in the form of water, sanitation, health and education projects which are funded through cocoa profits. It is a type of economic democracy in which members have a voice in cooperative business policy. Two Kuapa Kokoo members sit on the board of Day Chocolate which is part of the cooperative.

SERRV International has come a long way from helping World War II refugees sell their cuckoo clocks, but SERRV is still motivated by the same underlying principles of providing the economic tools for individuals to rebuild or strengthen their lives. For more information on SERRV go to our website at www.serrv.org and to buy Divine chocolate see www.serrv.org/divine.

Bob Chase, President
SERRV International

The World of Cocoa
GHANA
Goaso
Kumasi
Odaho
Accra
United States
United Kingdom
AFRICA
Ghana
TUNISIA
MOROCCO
ALGERIA
LIBYA
EGYPT
WESTERN SAHARA
MAURI-TANIA
MALI
NIGER
CHAD
SUDAN
ERITREA
DJIBOUTI
SOMALIA
ETHIOPIA
SENEGAL
THE GAMBIA
GUINEA-BISSAU
GUINEA
SIERRA LEONE
LIBERIA
CÔTE D'IVOIRE
BURKINA FASO
BENIN
TOGO
NIGERIA
CAMEROON
CENTRAL AFRICAN REPUBLIC
EQUITORIAL GUINEA
SÃO TOMÉ AND PRÍNCIPE
GABON
REPUBLIC OF THE CONGO
CABINDA
DEMOCRATIC REPUBLIC OF THE CONGO
UGANDA
KENYA
RWANDA
BURUNDI
TANZANIA
COMOROS
ANGOLA
ZAMBIA
MALAWI
MOZAMBIQUE
MADAGASCAR
ZIMBABWE
NAMIBIA
BOTSWANA
SWAZILAND
LESOTHO
SOUTH AFRICA
Beth N. Weisenborn

Odaho, Ghana, West Africa lies 40 kilometers, about 25 miles, southwest of the major city of Kumasi, in the Ashanti Region—one of the largest cocoa producing areas in the world. The village is four degrees north of the equator along a cocoa growing belt which wraps around the world from Brazil through West Africa to Indonesia.

There is one main dirt road cutting through the center of the village, with many trails and footpaths throughout carved by people, sheep, goats and dogs since the 1920's when Odaho was settled by a group of cocoa families from western Ghana.

There are some stone and brick structures here, but the construction method of choice is the ancient "waddle and daub" technique of lashing a bamboo frame together, covering the frame with mud plaster and then attaching a tin roof. Small shop-keepers sell their merchandise along the main road, and in the center of the village is the marketplace where fresh food is sold. Many families maintain garden plots along with their groves of cocoa trees.

It's hot here. This is equatorial Africa, and much of the work is done before the sun gets too high. When I arrive about 2 in the afternoon, I'm wringing wet with sweat—partially from the heat and partially from the fact I just realized one of my camera batteries is shot. I'm well aware the closest electricity is about ten miles in the other direction. I've just made the plunge into digital photography and I'm totally dependent on batteries for my camera and laptop computer. And now I'm down one battery with days before I can recharge.

But as the four-wheel drive vehicle crosses the second timber plank bridge and climbs the last hill into Odaho, the anxiety over a technical glitch subsides, and I start to feel at home. I always seem to distill a sense of comfort from the smell of smoke from a wood cook fire. I smell many fires here and start to feel a connection.

The main street of Odaho, Ghana is lined with small shops and homes and moves on due south to cocoa land at the edge of the village.

Paul Bempong, my friend and interpreter

There is a gathering of people of all ages waiting outside the Kuapa Kokoo storeroom and scales when I arrive. This is part of a large compound where some of that wood smoke is coming from. It is the home of Helena and Anthony Bempong and their extended family. They have previously agreed to let me "shadow" them for a week to document the lives of cocoa farmers.

We greet each other in the front of the building. I'm introduced to Helena, my hostess, and we walk to the side of the building to a large wooden door opening to a passageway leading to a courtyard. Helena introduces me to her son, Paul. We shake hands. I immediately like him. We chat for awhile, and he agrees to be my interpreter.

I also sense a connection with Helena. My first impression of her is a physically strong and attractive woman who smiles easily. We would smile many times later over what came next that day.

I've come to Ghana at an important time. The Annual General Meeting (AGM) of Kuapa Kokoo will be held in a few days. Delegates from all over Ghana will be attending the meeting and vote on important cooperative business. However, it's not the most fortuitous time for finding ripe cocoa being turned into dried beans for export. The primary harvest won't begin for another four months.

Helena Bempong at "The Harvest"

But in less than an hour of my arrival we walk through the village and are in the midst of a "staged" cocoa harvest at the nearest farm, all for my benefit. This is "the lean" or "the famine" time when the cocoa is still maturing. Not only is ripe cocoa scarce, so is cash, and it will be a long time before they'll see either.

Helena carries several ripe cocoa pods out from the village, and Peter Nsiah places one of them in the crotch of a tree limb so I can get a shot. Da-da! One yellow pod whizzes past Peter in his matching yellow polo shirt with brand new machete tucked under his arm. This is like an ad for maybe, "Cocoa Country"?

Peter Nsiah knocks the pod down.

Helena and Veronica

I'm struck with the hospitality of these people, and how they've gone out of their way to help me. In spite of the "set up", I will always remember a lovely portrait of a lovely woman wearing a nice shade of lipstick to match her crisp blouse, skirt and scarf looking as if she were having a picnic. Back at home, Veronica, Helena's 18-month-old granddaughter crawls into her grandmother's lap. There is a warmth and honesty between them which transcend the illusion of the "harvest". And even though I don't understand their *Twi* language, that first day we discover there is much to say with laughter which adds to our connection.

I meet another memorable woman my first day in the village—Mary Kwayie, Helena's sister-in-law. After the "cocoa harvest", Mary concentrates on the task of making a special laundry soap from last harvest's charred cocoa husks with a dash of lye she cooks in an iron cauldron. Mary's son, Samson, makes his supper roasting an ear of corn over the fire while his "Auntie" Helena stirs her batch of soap. And then I break out a music tape of Mr. Oduro's "Abiba" while Mary and her son, Paul, pick up the rhythm. Paul is named after his older cousin, Paul Bempong—my new friend—Helena's son. I'm a bit confused keeping everybody's name straight.

The center of family life for the Bempongs is a large open-air courtyard where all the cooking, eating and socializing take place. About nine sleeping rooms are arranged around the courtyard of the compound. Helena's daughter-in-law Joyce is in the foreground cutting chunks of cassava root, similar to potatoes. The men are sitting on stools and sharing their meal, eating with their right hand out of one pot. Emmanuel Opoku sits at the far right in the green shirt. Paul says he's the recorder of Kuapa Kokoo in Odaho—an important job. The children will eat after the men. Mary stands, looking over her pot of soap as her daughter, Agnes, also cuts cassava. Helena, sitting at the blue pail, continues to make soap.

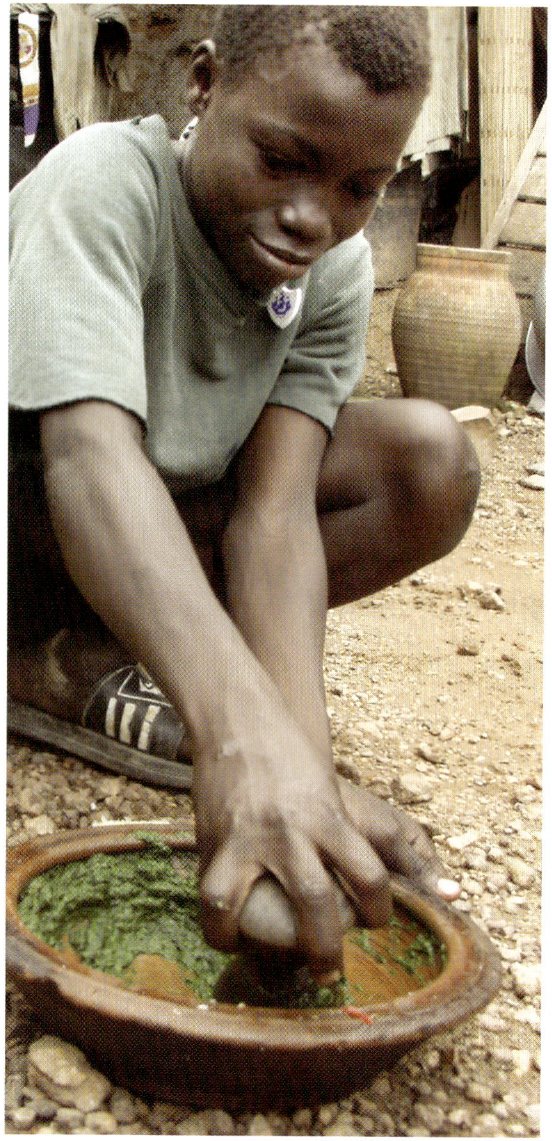

Mary's son, Paul Bempong, helps with the evening meal preparations.

I sense a closeness within this family. I think part of it comes through a bond that is formed with sharing the work load. The fact is, there's much work to be done, and it appears as if everyone shares the load. So far, it seems as if the women have the heaviest load of the domestic duties of food gathering, fire building, food preparation, cooking, water hauling, soap making and cleaning.

However, I notice while Mary is tending her fire and making soap, her son, Paul, squats beside a crockery type of mortar and pestle and grinds some vegetable in preparation for the evening meal. He's 14. No one tells him what to do. He knows his job.

I rarely see Anthony, Helena's husband. He has another role. He teaches elementary school in Odaho and in a nearby village. The family income is split between the sale of cocoa and his teaching job. He comes home after sundown, and as President of the Odaho Society of Kuapa, he spends many evenings listening to concerns from fellow cocoa farmers.

There is a quiet strength to Anthony—similar to what I sense his son, Paul has acquired. I can hear the 51-year old teacher-farmer at night counseling visitors in his tiny study, illuminated by a flicker of lamplight. I don't understand what is said, but I see farmers leave the room smiling. These are hard times with a scarcity of cash, but it appears as if Anthony has given them some hope. Before, Kuapa farmers had to tough it out on their own during this " lean" time. There seems to be bond among Kuapa farmers.

Helena's husband, Anthony, with his granddaughter, Veronica.

With no electricity in Odaho and kerosene used sparingly, night comes fast and people turn in for the day by nine o'clock or earlier. They'll be back up soon after first light around five in the morning. But one evening, with enough overhead illumination from a full moon, I see "the boys" gathered around Mary's son, Paul, who is reading in perfect English from one of his school papers. Paul wants to go on to the University to study science and medicine. "I want to come back to Odaho as a doctor so that my people will stay in good health," he tells me.

These boys are intelligent, and education is important to them, but in Ghana it's not free. A Kuapa farmer averages about 10 bags of cocoa each season which nets him about $670. That is his primary source of income for the year. School costs are the equivalent of $45 a year for secondary school with a boy's uniform costing $2 and girl's, $4. A cocoa farmer's "cutlass" or machete is about $3; bread, $.30 and a sack of corn which will help feed a family for one month is $6.25. Kerosene for lamplight is $1.30 a gallon. I can obviously see that life is hard in the village, but given a choice, I'm told that farmers would rather endure the hardships and uncertainty of the village and be able to grow much of their own food, than have to take their chances in the city selling bread by the roadside. And with the collective support of an organization like Kuapa Kokoo, the hardship is softened a bit for many farmers.

Philamena is the youngest of Helena and Anthony's five children. I watch her as she keeps an eye on the pot of boiling cassava root cooking over the wood fire in the small dirt floor room assigned for inside cooking.

Helena's youngest child, Philamena, watches over the evening meal cooking over an inside fire.

I'm struck with the thought that this 20-year old woman straddles two worlds: the traditional world of her home in Odaho tending fires, cooking, cleaning, helping on the cocoa farm and that world of her university studies and fulfilling her dream of becoming a doctor.

She has just entered her first year of university in Kumasi. Her tuition is about $125 a year with books and materials costing an additional $100 and food at $1.25 a day. Housing is approximately $20 a year. Philamena has taken a big step in leaving the traditional woman's role in the village for that of a profession. But part of her dream she says is to be able to return to the village and give something back to her people as a doctor. She comes from a tradition of cocoa farmers. Her grandfather came to Odaho more than 80 years ago to grow cocoa. Her parents have grown cocoa all their lives, and in spite of the hard life, cocoa has given Philamena the strength to reach beyond the village in order to bring something back home.

At 26, Paul Bempong is in a world of transition with one foot at home in his village and the other not certain where it will be planted while he awaits his assignment for one year of obligatory national service to his country. He hopes it will be in rural development. That's what he's been trained for, and what he received his degree in at the University in Kumasi. He is the son of cocoa farmers and knows the life is difficult. He wants life to be better for his people.

He tells me that Kuapa Kokoo is making things better by providing a fairer method of buying cocoa from the farmers. Traditional cocoa buying companies "cheat the farmer," he says. But he adds there's much more needed for people in the villages. "Clean water, sanitation—these are so important, and that's what I want to do to help." Kuapa Kokoo not only assists farmers with fair market incentives, it also reinvests in local villages to improve water quality, sanitation and encourages innovative women's projects such as soapmaking and traditional Kente cloth batik production.

He confesses he has another dream. "I want my privacy. There is absolutely no privacy here in the village. I love to read. I love to stay up late and read. It's difficult for me to do that here."

Just beyond his shoulder, behind the curtain, Paul's father is meeting with another farmer. Paul glances up from his papers and says, "We have much to be thankful for here. I just want to help make it better."

Paul Bempong finds a bit of quiet time for reading by lamplight

It's her hands. That's what I first remember about Afua Nyame when I look back to our meeting at Helena's home. At 80, she's the oldest working cocoa farmer in Odaho. Actually, she lives in a tiny settlement with her two younger sisters at the edge of their cocoa farm just across the Subin River, about an hour's walk west of Odaho. Afua stops by the the Bempongs to tend to some cocoa business with Kuapa recorder "Emma" Opoku, but quickly falls into a lively conversation with her old friend and fellow cocoa farmer, Helena, along with Philamena. I sit at the old woman's feet and am taken in by her hands, and then her laughter. I have no idea what the women are discussing. But it's obviously funny.

There's something else about Afua. The beauty of her leathered hands draws me closer, and then I sense something deeper to my connection with the old woman—something I don't quite understand.

Afua Nyame stops by to chat with Helena and Philamena and share a funny story with her cocoa farmer friends.

I love to wander back alleys and strange streets, wherever I am. I've always just wandered, all over the world. In Odaho I wander Sunday morning and chat with Margaret Asiamah. I find her sweeping the road in front of her home. That afternoon I pass by her home again and learn about split bamboo fish traps from she and her husband, " B.K. " The two are working out front, lashing together splits of bamboo making their traps when Paul and I walk up. The cocoa farmer-fisherman explains both ends of the trap have a tapered opening for the fish to swim into. But the fish can't figure out how to swim back out, and they end up in fish stew for supper, which is nice when food is more scarce at this time of the cocoa cycle.

B.K. and Margaret Asiamah lash their bamboo fish traps and share lively conversation on their front porch.

B.K. Asiamah, cocoa farmer—fisherman

I think if I only had the time to go fishing with B.K. and understand his stories. For now I'm thankful for an afternoon sun highlighting this old man's face, glistening over a powerful left forearm. I wonder which is more profound: the aesthetic of the traps he and his wife make, the strength in his forearm or the dignity in his face?

On down the main street from B.K. and Margaret's home is one of four village waterwells or "blowpipes" as Paul calls them. In many ways it is the heart of Odaho as it is in any village. I live just up the path from this one at the south edge of town. It's always a place of laughter and conversation, and I'm usually a subject of curiosity: tall, bald, white, funny clothes, funny thing hanging around my neck, occasionally stumbling on the rocks.

Traditionally, water was carried from a nearby stream, but there was always the risk of contamination. But now Kuapa Kokoo takes some of its profits from the international sale of cocoa and plows the money back into rural development projects such as village "blowpipes", providing deep wells with clean water.

Fresh, clean water from the "blowpipe" is important to the general health of villagers.

After a Ghanaian pleasantly greets you with "*akwaba"* (welcome), you will typically be asked, "What is your mission?" My mission is to find out as much about cocoa as I can, but this is my fourth day in Ghana, and so far I've seen cocoa stuck back up in a tree for a "photo op" along with lots of empty bamboo racks where cocoa will be drying in four months. However. I've been taken in by an extended family of cocoa farmers who laugh with me, feed me and seem to be going about their daily living as if I'm part of their family too. And although cocoa cultivation photos are scarce, I have an abundance of images of village and family life. But today is an important day in the cocoa story. Helena, Paul and I are going off to the Annual General Meeting (AGM) of Kuapa Kokoo to join about 2,000 delegates from all over Ghana who will meet in Goaso.

We will be gone from the village for three days, and there still are chores to do at home.

Helena is all dressed up in a traveling dress as she finishes the last of the breakfast dishes with some help from Veronica, the youngest Bempong. Helena enjoys the company and likes the fact that Veronica wants to help. There's a brief moment when Veronica seems stuck in her work which amuses Granny. And then the two have a moment of affection before the truck arrives to start our journey.

The pick-up truck from Kuapa is waiting in front of the society warehouse where passengers to various destinations are waiting. Some are catching a ride to a nearby village. Others will go on to the main road about 15 miles away, then take a van into Kumasi. Others like Helena, Paul and I will ride to the Kuapa district office then board a hired bus to Goaso, about three hours from Odaho. It's a long journey, and two days of meetings, but it gives cocoa farmers like Helena the opportunity to have a direct vote in the business of their cooperative. In four months, the area where Helena walks will be a carpet of cocoa drying in the sun. The red scales in the distance will have held tons of dried beans ready for international shipment during the final phase of the harvest. For now, the Annual General Meeting, represents another kind of harvest relatively new to cocoa farmers.

Helena walks in front of the Kuapa warehouse to catch her ride to the Annual General Meeting. The red scales in the background will be busy weighing cocoa during the harvest.

Before the liberalization of cocoa marketing, farmers were at the mercy of unscrupulous buying companies and a fickle world cocoa market. That changed in 1993 when Kuapa Kokoo was founded to allow farmers the chance to be actual shareholders in their buying company. The AGM is the shareholders meeting and delegates are sent from each Kuapa society to represent concerns from all farmer members.

It's a type of economic democracy, and from the the enthusiasm I find at the AGM, members are quite proud of Kuapa.

Delegates to the Kuapa Kokoo Annual General Meeting celebrate the occasion with a march to the meeting grounds where they will vote on important cooperative business. Nearly 2,000 cocoa farmers from across Ghana attend the AGM.

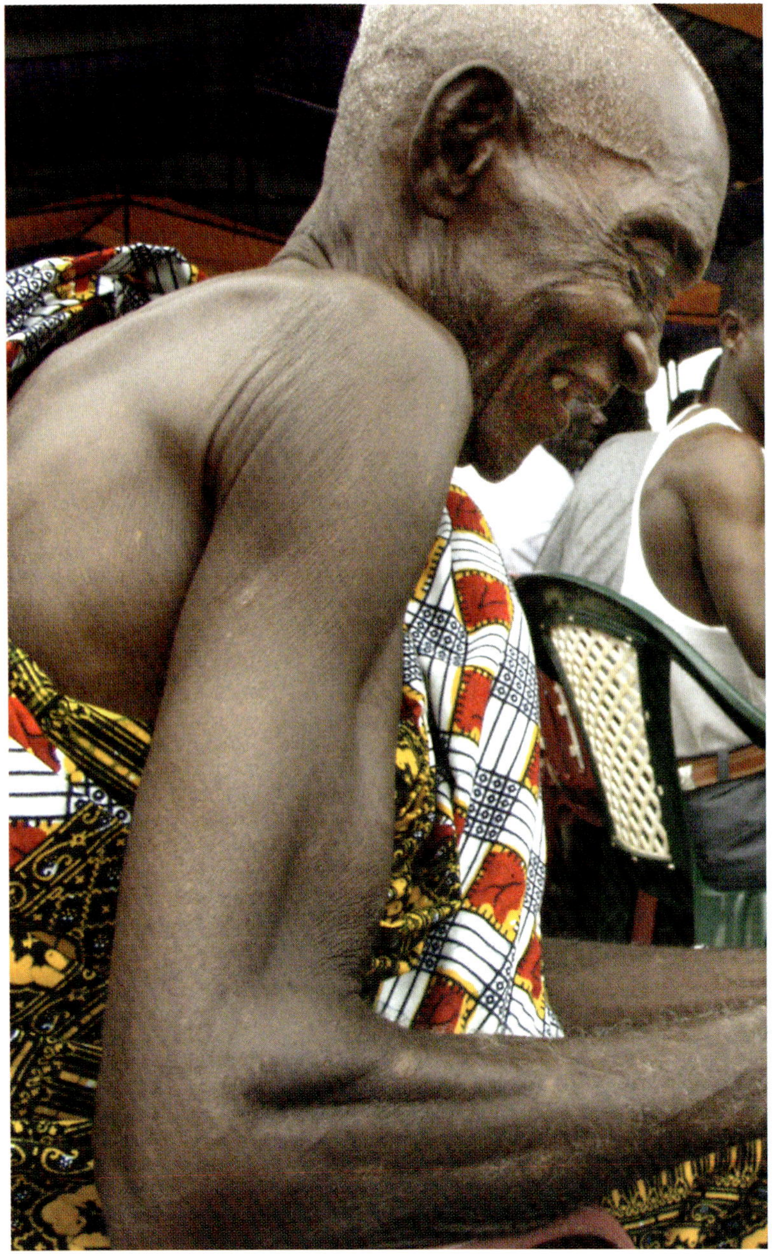

I don't know his name. He's an old cocoa farmer, and we became friends on the way to the general meeting all because of one tiny piece of chocolate. . .

Helena, Paul and I have been waiting over an hour for the bus to take our group the rest of the way to the AGM meeting grounds another two hours away. I see the old man is getting impatient—even angry—the longer we wait. The old farmer speaks loudly to somebody who looks like he might be a Kuapa official. I see the old man storm off, mumbling angrily to himself. I catch up to him, but he's uncertain of me. I reach in my vest and pull out one tiny, chocolate egg I'd brought from the States. I hand it to him. He peels back the foil, pops the chocolate in his mouth and his scowl turns to a broad smile. We shake hands, and our connection is sealed—by a little chocolate egg.

I see my friend several times the next day at the AGM dressed in his traditional robe and make his portrait—smiling. Every time I see him he's smiling. I think how in some ways the essence of this large gathering of farmers is about joy and pride. To put it bluntly, these farmers were getting "ripped off" before Kuapa came along giving farmers like my old friend a fair and guaranteed market for their cocoa.

Soon, the Day Chocolate Company was incorporated into Kuapa. The company purchased cocoa from Kuapa farmers, including the old man, and turned it into chocolate bars and tiny eggs. One of those eggs brought two strangers together . A circle is connected which all started in an old man's hands the moment he planted one cocoa seedling many years ago. The size of the world just shrank a tiny bit.

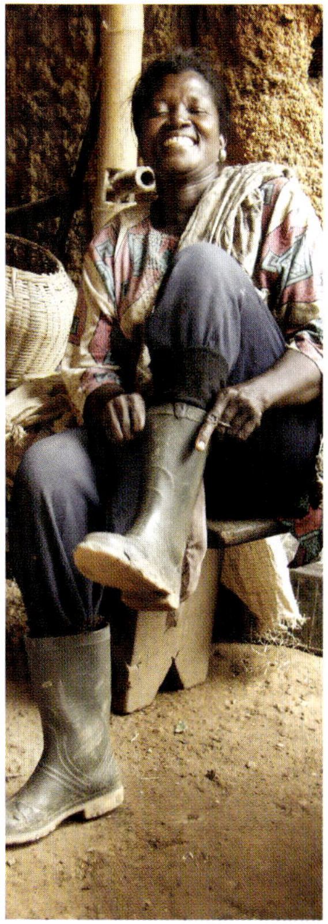

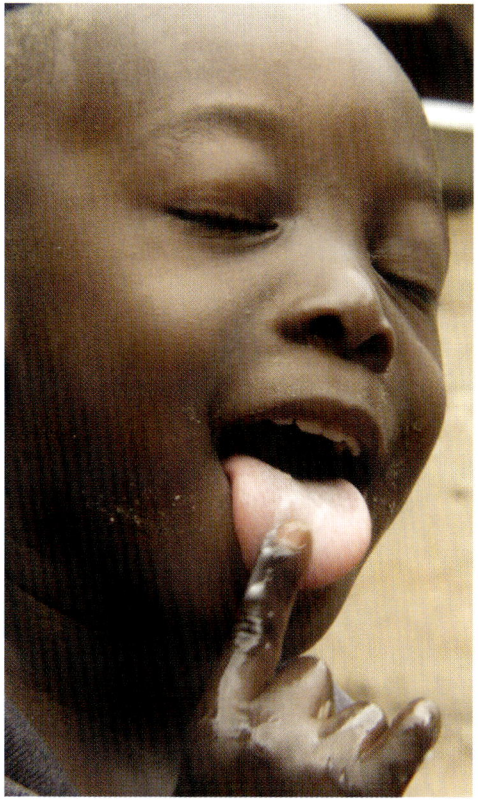

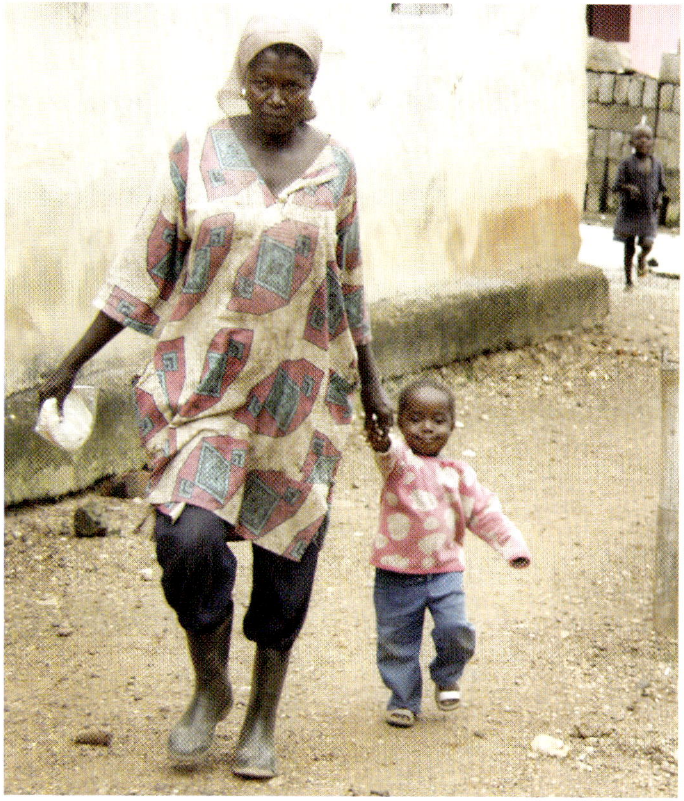

We arrive back in Odaho late Wednesday evening. I have one full day left in the village, but still have no real photos of cocoa farm work. I lay out my problem to Paul that night when we get home. His solution is "baby cocoa", as he calls the young seedlings that need to be planted. The next morning I explain my problem to Helena and how important it is for me to get photos of her working on the farm. I know she is tired and still recovering from the trip to the AGM. My friend agrees to go to the farm and plant seedlings. She just needs to slip on her Wellington rubber boots and round up Richard and Veronica who have just finished their oatmeal and are off playing. Mary is staying home today and will look after the children.

It takes about five years for a cocoa tree to mature enough to produce ripe fruit that can be harvested for the production of chocolate. I came across the earliest stages of cocoa cultivation my first day in Odaho. Kwaku Minteh and his son, Kofi Amakye were sitting on the ground filling plastic bags with sand, to "nest" or plant cocoa seeds which would become cocoa tree seedlings. Most farmers have their own nursery beds. Helena's seedlings grow behind the family home, shaded by a bamboo mat roof.

Helena loads about a dozen seedlings on a large platter on her head. Paul and I follow behind her walking about an hour out to her farm. She maintains a long stride going up and down the lush hills, past small cornfields, through other cocoa groves and over logs across small streams Cocoa is grown on the transitional land lying between the tropical rainforest and open grasslands.

Helena walks through the lush countryside on the way to her farm as she carries a load of cocoa seedlings which need to be planted.

We reach the 10-acre hillside farm by mid day with the temperature approaching 100 degrees. Helena looks up the partially cleared land and decides where she wanted to plant. But before any actual planting can begin she prays. She rests her planting staff across her leg and focuses on the ground making the sign of the cross. Paul told me later his mother "Thanked God for leading us safely to the farm. She prayed that He, almighty God, would protect us from any possible accident so that when we returned home from the work safely, she could give Him all the glory and honor."

And then Helena stabs the earth—pries back the soil and begins planting.

Helena uses the tools cocoa farmers have used for centuries: a digging staff to pry back the earth and her hands to place the cocoa seedling in the ground.

Paul moves on up the hillside and digs out more planting holes for his mother who carefully places a young seedling in each hole. The surrounding plantain and banana trees will provide the needed shade for the developing trees. For now the big question Helena has—the question all farmers everywhere have—will the rains come at the right time, in the right amount, and will the young seedlings be spared disease, insects or gnawing animals? Helena knows she's going to loose some of these seedlings along the way. If all goes well, the "baby cocoa" will be producing mature fruit in about five years.

She takes a rare break from the work, sits on the soft leaf litter and stares down through a grove of mature cocoa trees. Her farm ends at the bottom of the hill where there's a tract of land covered with heavy brush. She and Anthony have thought about buying that land and adding to these 10 acres, but it will require a tremendous amount of effort to clear, and there's much work already in maintaining what they have.

Helena gets up and surveys the progress of the ripening cocoa. There's still about four months before the harvest and some of the lime green pods are starting to turn "wine red" which will be followed by the golden hue of the mature pods.

She walks on through the grove and stops at the base of an oil palm tree to pick palm nuts. She knows I'm leaving tomorrow, and she wants to make me some of her palm nut soup for supper. Most of what the family eats is grown here on the farm. She adds the red nuts to the pile of cassava roots and plantain on the platter.

She raises the load of vegetables, and we head home.

Helena is greeted at home by her nephew, Badu, Mary's son, who helps his "Auntie" with the load of fresh vegetables from the farm. She doesn't stop. She hasn't stopped all day. She got up before sunrise, after a late-night return from the Kuapa meeting. She worked all day on the farm which included a six-mile roundtrip walk carrying a heavy load. I realize I've seen her take one swig of water all day, and I've been through one canteen and one liter bottle. She immediately puts down the platter with Badu's help and goes to her interior cooking place. There are still a few coals from breakfast, but the fire needs some help, so she walks down to Mary's fire and retrieves some flaming coals to get her dinner fire rolling. At last she does get to sit, but she's still working, sitting at her favorite stool as she slices tomatoes and onions. The palm nuts are put in boiling water to soften, and then she mashes the nuts in a mortar and pestle to separate out the pulp from the seeds and skin. The mash is put back in the pot with the fresh onions, tomatoes and peppers to simmer. The reddish stew is served over steamed rice. It's delicious. The only distasteful part of the meal is the thought that this will be my last with this family.

The next morning, the Kuapa storeroom is empty except for a few jute cocoa sacks scattered on some pallets as I wait for my ride to Kumasi and begin my journey home. There's a slight aroma of cocoa lingering in the air which has soaked into the plaster from many harvests when this place, I imagine, has been filled with sacks of cocoa. A poster of Jesus hangs on the far wall. I don't understand the message. I'm not Catholic. But many of these people are. They have a deep faith. These tillers of the soil carry that faith every day as they pick their corn, cut their cassava, plant their "baby cocoa" all the while giving thanks for a safe journey through life, in spite of incredible odds.

Appia Kofi (left) and his brother Mark Gyan begin another day by starting their morning breakfast fire.

I feel as if a thousand miles lies between this linoleum-covered, chipped paint hotel room in suburban Kumasi, Ghana and my adopted family just down the road in Odaho. It's almost two o'clock in the morning. I've been gone from the village 12 hours. The only sound comes from an ancient air conditioner pumping out the smell of mildew and spent cigarettes.

I'm like the lambs I would hear just beyond my bed, bleating out into the night searching for their mothers. I hear no crickets. No bullfrogs. No call from that mystically-colored bird with green shirt, black belly and red cape who drank nectar with its long bill from the giant red hibiscus tree just beyond that same bed. No rooster crows outside this place. There are no first morning prayers from my Muslim neighbor—no sounds from his baby boy. I hear no clatter of cooking pots from last night's supper being washed by the young mother who sings happy sounding songs of things I wish I knew—songs being learned by the infant strapped snuggly to her mother's back. There is no palm nut soup being prepared by a sweat-soaked woman moving—always moving—through another day of endless work.

But most striking is the fact I can no longer smell the smoke triggering the comforting memories. The boys up the path have a few more hours of sleep before they need to start today's breakfast fire. It was their fire my first morning in Odaho which drew me in and helped me make another connection with that place. Appia Kofi and his older brother Mark Gyan couldn't help laughing when they saw some strange, bald-headed white man with the side of his face in the dust blowing into their fire to help get it going. Here in the city it's the absence of smoke which tells me I'm not at home. The smoke is part of the soul of the village I cannot find here.

From West Bengal to northern Thailand, the Philippines to Nicaragua, Sudan, Vietnam, Dominican Republic and south India—it's the smell of smoke from a morning breakfast fire which trails off and leads my memory to the fires of my boyhood canoeing the Canadian wilderness. It was the smoke from the fires I just left behind which told me I had a home in a beautiful place among beautiful people.

The separation anxiety is heightened by the fact I know I have only begun to understand the story of these people. The story I need to tell is like a wine-red cocoa pod with four months before turning golden. I shall return for the harvest.

"Mr. Phil. You kept your promise. You came back," Emmanuel Opoku yells as we pass through his village, ten minutes before Odaho. "Of course I did, Emma. I had to come back and keep you straight," I yell at him. The Kuapa Kokoo recorder laughs, "Oh, Mr. Phil. Mr. Phil," as we shake hands.

Emma and I had become good friends back in July even though I kidded him about following me around like a dog at first. "I had to keep you straight, Mr. Phil," he would laugh.

"Hey, Emma. Did you find any cocoa," I jokingly asked him remembering that first day when Pete stuck the cocoa pod back up in a tree.

"Oh, Mr. Phil. You go look. I'll be there later."

My driver heads on out of the village and drives down through the savannah, crosses that second timber plank bridge, up the hill and into Odaho.

My nose is the first to notice things have changed. The smell of wood fires has been replaced by the aroma of vinegar. At first I thought the women were cooking something unusual, but then it hits me that it must be acetic acid from the fermenting and drying cocoa beans I see everywhere. And the Kuapa storeroom is loaded with sacks of cocoa waiting to be trucked out. Things have definitely changed.

The Kuapa Kokoo warehouse in Odaho is filling up with jute sacks of dried cocoa beans, each weighing exactly 62.4 kilograms or about 138 pounds.

Cocoa—it's everywhere. There's a river of cocoa flowing from the Kuapa warehouse. "The lean" is gone. The harvest is here. This village has been transformed since I left four months ago. It's been injected with celebration. Around the corner Kojo Ose spreads out a batch of newly fermented cocoa beans from Mary's farm. This whole village is grinning.

They're dancing in the streets—even a young man with handicapped legs has thrown away his cane and is on the ground dancing to the "High Life" beat pounding from the massive speakers set up across from the marketplace. They've trucked in a generator to power the sound system brought in by a DJ from Kumasi with crates of music CD's.

I even jump in, that first night, but almost get a dislocated hip doing "the bump" with a cocoa lady. Paul Bempong just shakes his head and laughs.

It's not only the harvest, there's a traditional three-day funeral celebration for a departed cocoa farmer. The circle of life has enveloped this village. An honored cocoa farmer moves out of this life and into a new one, while a new harvest full of abundance and hope pushes aside a period of lean and sacrifice.

I get caught in the middle of the women's march during the funeral ceremony and find myself nearly overrun by the joyous celebrants.

Paul Bempong

For the here and now, Odaho is on fire with celebration.

The funeral for a departed cocoa farmer is a time of celebration for these women who fan out and march down the main street of Odaho during the three-day event. Ghanaian funerals are elaborate and expensive which can add to the financial burden of a family.

. . .And there's celebration going on in the New Testament Assembly of Odaho as Akua Hagger slaps her tambourine and sings out while her infant Adjaw Pomah is strapped on for a jubilant ride.

Inside the Bempong compound, I have a fond reunion with my old friends Helena and her sister-in-law, Mary. The middle age cocoa farmers are running around like a couple of school girls wearing new scarves I've brought from the States. There's a harvest of new cocoa, pretty scarves and old friends. Part of my return is prompted by these two. The other is hanging in trees an hour east of here at Helena's cocoa farm.

Helena has traded her new scarf for a familiar work scarf. The brightly colored jersey is replaced by a faded tee shirt stained by a mixture of cocoa and sweat. There is some relief under this canopy of shade of the cocoa grove, but it's still about 100 degrees down here. Helena is hunting ripe cocoa pods. She looks like a wily hunter prowling this hillside with her 10-foot bamboo pole.

There's a flat, sharpened piece of metal lashed to the end of the pole. She spots a ripe pod and deftly thrusts the blade at just the right point and slices the stem to "pluck" the cocoa pod which falls to the ground.

Four months ago I left the cocoa story on this hillside with Helena looking down through this grove wondering what kind of harvest she was going to have. The rains were a bit late last spring, so the quantity of ripe cocoa is a little less. She can't really concern herself about that now. She moves along the leaf litter picking up the golden pods, collecting them in her gathering basket much the way thousands of harvests have been gathered. An ancient rhythm is being played out on this hillside which trails back to a time before there was cocoa in Africa—back to a Pre-Columbian civilization in South America where the harvesting tools were probably very similar to what Helena uses: a pole with a cutting blade or stone attached, a basket and a pair of hands.

Helena moves along the hillside and collects the ripe cocoa pods from the ground putting them in a gathering basket.

It doesn't take long for the cocoa to mound up at a central collecting site where Helena and Paul sit at one large pile and begin the process of opening the pods and scooping out the fleshy, white beans inside.

Each mature cocoa tree has an average of about 30 pods each season. A tree may have thousands of tiny white blossoms, but only a relative handful get pollinated and become seed pods because insects have a difficult time finding their way inside the blossoms. Once pollinated, cocoa is susceptible to disease and harmful insects which take their toll on about 30 percent of the cocoa crop worldwide each season.

A mound of freshly "plucked" cocoa pods dwarfs Paul and his mother as he uses his cutlass to make several slashes into a pod while Helena strips the cocoa seeds into a basket.

Mary's daughter Agnes uses her cutlass to make several slashes into the cocoa husk which she pries slightly open with the blade before passing it on. The husk is fully opened revealing the cluster of seeds which are covered with a white mucilage all attached to a spine. The beans are stripped away into another basket. Occasionally a few of the sweet beans might get sucked on as a treat.

There are about 40 seeds to a pod and 30 pods to a tree. When dried, that's enough cocoa beans to make four, 3.5-ounce bars of chocolate.

The "cocoa bones", or mass of cocoa seeds, are stripped away from a soft spine inside the pod. Agnes, Mary's daughter, uses her cutlass to slash open a pod to get to the fresh cocoa seeds.

Four months ago when cocoa was rather scarce, Helena carried out four ripe pods for "the harvest". That might have made a couple of chocolate "kisses". Now as Mary hauls off another load of fresh beans and walks between the piles of empty cocoa husks and pods to be stripped, I can't imagine how this all computes to chocolate. I do know this is a tremendous amount of work.

The cocoa grove is filling up with empty husks in the foreground which will be burned after the harvest with the ash from the fire used for soap. Some of last years charred husks are in a pile to the right. Mary walks between the mounds of new cocoa with a load of freshly stripped cocoa, while her son, Samson, throws an empty pod on the pile and other workers continue working through the pile of cocoa behind him.

Badu and his brother, Samson, have filled up another basket of fresh cocoa, and Mary comes by to retrieve the cocoa from her sons. The mound is growing while Mary and Agnes dump the heavy load on the main pile which will later be covered over and left in the grove to ferment.

As I watch Helena scoop out more cocoa, my mind flashes back again to the day we met four months ago, and the "lovely" portrait I made of her. This is the portrait of Helena I came back for. Her face is covered with sweat from hard work and radiates joy. It's truly lovely.

Paul dumps another load of fresh cocoa then spreads the sticky mass of seeds out on banana leaves.

Mary breaks away from hauling cocoa and uses her bamboo pole to "pluck" several more leaves. Along with the harvest, she's been tending her cook fire preparing a meal of cassava she cut earlier. She spreads out some of the banana leaves as a type of tablecloth for the meal. She uses the other leaves she's cut to cover over the pile of fresh cocoa.

Once all the cocoa has been "plucked" for the day, the seeds stripped from the pods and the pile of fresh cocoa completed, Mary covers over the massive mound with banana leaves to begin the critical stage of the harvest—the fermentation of the beans. The fresh cocoa has a sweet, fruity taste and the fermentation, which takes about five days, gives the beans the distinctive, chocolate flavor. That taste is enhanced months later when the dried beans are roasted at a chocolate processing factory. During the fermentation, the white mucilage covering is reduced to a sticky coating which smells of vinegar—the aroma I first noticed yesterday when I arrived in Odaho. It's an important smell and all part of the process of turning a seed into a bean. Some of the seeds are set aside to germinate, sprout and grow into seedlings of future cocoa trees.

Before leaving the farm, the women gather any fresh cocoa which might have fallen out of the gathering baskets and throw all the empty husks to the pile.

Mary takes a swig of water from a cup she fashioned from a banana leaf, and heads back to the village.

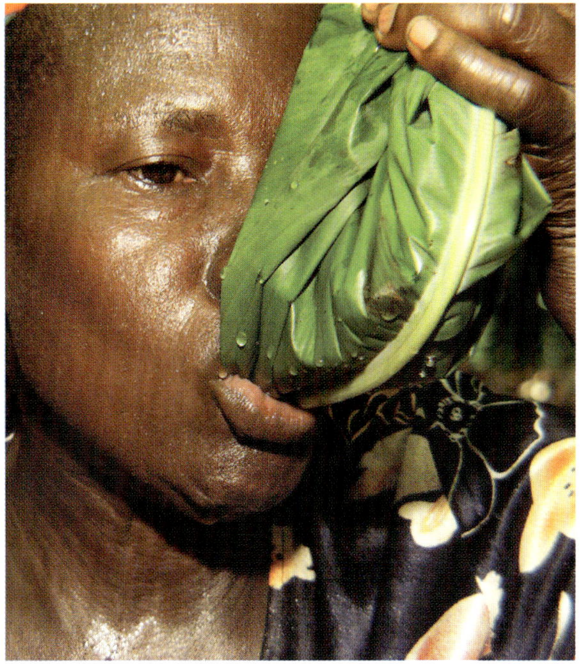

I can't sleep. Between the full moon, a chorus of amorous bullfrogs and the heat, I've had enough tossing and turning. I walk though the night to investigate the singing and find the lads lined up in a large mud puddle just at the south edge of the village. I record the singing on my cassette recorder and watch the moon slide across the sky and illuminate the scattering of Onyina trees, standing watch some 60 to 80 feet in the air over the blanket of cocoa groves and hillside cornfields laying at their feet. I never tire of admiring the majestic Onyina—by moonlight, sun-light or the light of my memory. The moon guides me through the village back to my room where a few lambs are still looking for their mothers.

The next morning the Onyina trees that were covered in moonlight last night are now shrouded in a marvelously eerie fog which drifted in while I drifted off to sleep. I've walked out the road to check on my male chorus in the mud. They're silent. I only hear the crunching footfalls of three men emerging from the fog, each carrying their load of fermented cocoa beans on their heads. They're flanked by faint silhouettes of Onyina trees, cloaked in this misty, morning fog looking like a scene out of a Japanese screen painting.

Onyina trees stab through
morning's cloak—fog whispers
to cocoa men and muted frogs.

I'm able to get two exposures off before they pass. We smile, and I try my new phrase Emma taught me in the native *Twi* language: **"Ninyinaa efe!"** and one of them replies, **"Efe."** It's pronounced "**nin-ya-NAY**", with a rising pitch on the long "**NAY**", and then the "**efe**" is spoken as if you were going to say **effect**, but the **ct** gets cut off. Literally it translates, "This place, with all of its people, all of its animals, its trees and flowers and grass, its smells and sounds—everything is beautiful."

I'm not certain if my friends would actually find beauty in the work they did yesterday, sweating in the cocoa grove all day, "plucking", husking, stripping, hauling, walking, and then getting home to tend cook fires, prepare the evening meal, wash dishes, sweep and finally roll out a mat on the dirt in the courtyard and find rest under the stars, away from the heat of the sleeping rooms.

I have the luxury as an observer to find beauty in their toil. Actually, to find beauty in the spirit I sense wringing from their toil—as much as their sweat. I see beauty in the simplicity of their way of life and the unspoken reverence they share for the rhythms of their work and the rhythms of the earth. There's even beauty in the sound of these footfalls on red dirt and gravel as three cocoa men carry their loads back home—beauty in the silence of a hundred sleeping bullfrogs.

Ninyinaa efe!

There's a river of cocoa moving from the trees to the fermenting piles, and now to the drying racks of split bamboo in the village where Mary's oldest son Mathew spreads out a fresh load of beans while the "inspectors" discuss important matters. Mathew not only tends the drying cocoa, he also checks on the fire under his fish soup. Helping out with the constant job of stirring the drying beans is Isaac Amankwaa (left).

The equatorial afternoon sun beats down on Mary's drying cocoa beans (left) as she stirs through a section of the carpet of cocoa that will soon be ready to take to the scales for weighing. Helena examines the progress of a rack of her beans, checking for quality and dryness. It takes five to seven days for the beans to thoroughly dry. When the beans are fermenting in a pile in the grove, the white mucilage covering decomposes and leaves a sticky coating. The coating is reduced to a dry, reddish-brown shell during the drying process on the racks.

Afua Nyame works alone stirring her cocoa as it dries on bamboo racks in her tiny settlement. The old woman's "waddle and daub" mud plaster home is just behind her.

Emma, Paul and I have walked out to Afua Nyame's home west of Odaho. Emma feels badly Afua has walked all the way in to the Kuapa headquarters to see him several times this week to check on getting paid for her cocoa. He knows that cash is scarce for the old woman, as it is for many of the farmers. There is a delay with the banks in Kumasi where the main office of Kuapa gets its funds for distribution to all the Kuapa societies in Ghana for paying the farmers. Emma also knows that some of her cocoa money goes to buying her own medicine. There is no free health care nor prescription drug plans in Ghana. Emma wants to make sure she's all right.

When we arrive, Afua is stirring through the cocoa she and her sisters recently brought into the family drying racks next to her small, mud-plastered home. She's glad to see us, and has the same laugh I remember photographing four months ago, sitting at her feet while she chatted with Helena and Philamena. I will always remember her hands, the color of dried cocoa.

Something else I will never forget. I make a portrait of Afua leaning against the side of her home with her left hand resting on a small bag of cocoa. Looking through my viewfinder I notice that the stretched, leathered skin over her sternum is bulging in and out, rhythmically. I can actually see her heart beat. And then I recall Emma had told me last summer that Afua has "chest pains. She needs her medicine."

Back then she also needed to borrow the equivalent of about $12. Although Afua is a member of Kaupa, she is not a member of Kuapa's credit union which would allow her to borrow against her deposits when cash is scarce. It would cost Afua about $1.25 to register with the credit union. Then she would need to deposit about $6 in her account to borrow money later.

I considered $12 a fair trade for all the food and lodging I was receiving from my friends. Besides, the picture of Afua's leathered hands was priceless. I gave Emma the money, but instructed him not to tell Afua who the donor was.

Emma tells me he feels badly about Afua's situation. She lives entirely off the cash from her cocoa. "Now there's a delay with the banks, and the old woman needs her money. It's not really Kuapa's fault. It's the banks. But the farmers still need their cash," he says.

Cocoa farmer Osci Bowbi watches as a Kuapa worker hauls a sack of his cocoa to the scales. Emma (right) checks the scales making sure each sack contains 62.4 kilograms of dried beans.

There's more cocoa to weigh, and Emma and his helpers are back at it early in the morning. A big producer, Osci Bowbi, comes in with four large sacks of beans that are perfectly dry, according to Emma. Many times, the beans have to be finished off for a bit of additional drying in front of the Kuapa warehouse because Emma is trying to get the best quality of bean with a minimum of moisture content. Osci has three sacks weighing in at 64 kilos and one at 53. The actual weight of his cocoa will be credited in his record book, and then each of the four sacks will be adjusted so that each weighs exactly 62.4 kilograms—about 138 pounds. The sacks are hauled inside the warehouse, sewn shut and made ready for shipment. Osci is 71 years old and has been working cocoa for 25 years. He's also head of the Kuapa's credit union in Odaho. Last year he says he had a total harvest of 33 sacks. He expects a little less this year since the rains were off in the spring. Most Odaho farmers average about 10 sacks in a season.

A carpet of cocoa rolls out in front of the Kuapa Kokoo warehouse as workers spread the beans for further drying. Another worker (right) scoops through the mass to make certain the beans dry evenly. The beans will then be shoveled into sacks for final weighing before shipment.

Kwame Dapaah hauls a sack of dried cocoa weighing more than 100 pounds to the scales at Kuapa where it will be evened out to weigh the required 62.4 kilograms. Kwame, 15, works after school and on the weekends helping his father, Kofi Krah, at Kuapa during the harvest. They also squeeze in time to work their own cocoa. Kwame says he wants to finish his education and then work as a cocoa farmer.

Kuapa Kokoo workers haul the 138-pound cocoa sacks out of the warehouse and heave them up into a dump truck which will deliver them to a central depot. They will then be moved to port for shipment.

Another load of cocoa pulls away from the Kuapa warehouse, and Emma climbs in the cab to ride the truck down to the depot about ten miles away. He says he's concerned about the situation with the banks in Kumasi, and he wants to go to Kuapa headquarters to see if he can get the funds to pay his farmers. It's customary to give a farmer the option of deferring payment for his cocoa with the incentive of receiving a slight bonus for each sack of cocoa. But Emma knows the bank delays are causing extra hardship on the farmers, and he wants to help them. A few large growers can afford to wait, but many are short of cash. Others, like Helena, have side enterprises to bring in extra cash.

Helena not only raises cocoa, she also buys bolts of sewing cloth and shoes from a friend in Kumasi on short-term credit, then sells the merchandise in Odaho at a slight profit. She repays her friend and then brings back more resale items to the village. It helps keep the Bempongs a little bit ahead when the cocoa cash hasn't come in. It also gives Helena a chance to enjoy a break from tedious cocoa work and, at the same time, socialize with old friends.

Helena passes the warehouse of another cocoa buying company while she makes her rounds selling cloth. She moves on past a bicycle repair shop where one of the village chiefs, Osci Kwaku, lives.

Helena has already made a sale of cloth to Rose Ampongsan who takes a long look at a pair of dress shoes with a miniature plastic rose encased in the clear plastic heel. The shoes get a lot of interest, but no purchase.

Two cocoa farmers do some hard bargaining over the dress shoes, but when it's all over, Ama Osaa is pleased with her purchase of cloth without the shoes. And Helena is happy with another sale she can mark down in her ledger. When Ama's cocoa money comes she'll pay her friend. Helena continues her route through the villages and passes my home.

The cocoa lady has had a good day selling cloth and making some extra income. In fact, the sales are so good, she decides to buy the dress shoes herself.

I, too, have entered the local economy through my friend Margaret Asiamah who tends the drying rack stirring through the cocoa beans she and B.K. have brought in from their farm.

Also drying are two bandannas that were wringing wet with my sweat yesterday. I hire Margaret to do my wash and usually see her every day with a new load of clothes. Unfortunately I always seem to miss B.K. who is out working his cocoa from early in the morning to late in the evening. There's no time to see his fish traps in use.

Back at my room I hear someone near the hibiscus. It's two boys about 15 or 16. One boy is carrying a small, plastic bucket filled with partially dried cocoa beans. There is a large fruit on top looking something like a heart. One boy says, "It is for you." I ask them what the strange fruit is. He replies, referring to the cocoa, "They are seeds of hope." I ask, "Are you giving them to me?" He says, "No, just the apple. You buy cocoa."

I'm moved by the gift of the apple. I think fast. "I really don't need any cocoa, but I do need water. Will you take my jugs to the blowpipe and fill them with water, and then I'll pay you 5,000 cedis?" They're back in ten minutes with fresh water for me, and they have about 75 cents more than they did 20 minutes ago. Intentional or not, the boys' gift of heart-shaped fruit is added to all the other gifts of the heart I've received in this village.

I see men dressed in funeral robes just up the alley where Helena passed yesterday selling her cloth. They look important. I investigate. They are village elders—actually a Senior Assistant Chief and an Assistant Chief. In traditional Ghanaian culture, it is customary for a visitor to a village to meet with the Chief and present him with a bottle of Schnapps. I introduce myself and apologize through Paul about my oversight on the Schnapps. They accept, but make a suggestion so that I can correct my cultural indiscretion.

Paul and I excuse ourselves and come back with a bottle of Schnapps I find in a bar a few minutes away. The tradition calls for the Chief to pour a bit of Schnapps on the ground, and then everyone shares in the drinking. It doesn't quite go that way. At first they just want pictures, but I notice the bottle cap is still secured. So the Senior Assistant Chief, Osie Kwaku, holds out his glass and convinces the others to open the bottle and pour. Assistant Chief Yaw Gamfi has a few words for Chief Osie, but then is glad to do the honors and pours his friend about two fingers of Schnapps. And that makes Chief Osie very happy.

But it leaves me confused. No one wants to waste the Schnapps on the ground nor the lips of their visitor with the camera. I think I've just been taken on a Ghanaian "snipe hunt."

Agnes has just brought in a load of fresh tomatoes from Mary's farm when I find she and Josephine sorting through the collection. Agnes divides up her metal platter with pieces of kindling wood and dried corncobs to create small cells to hold the tomatoes which she'll sell at the market for some extra cash.

Emma taught me how to say the words, "Ninyinaa efe." I say them out loud and Agnes pauses in her work and smiles at me. I wonder if she knows how beautiful her hands are with water glistening on fingers touching red tomatoes—the same fingers I saw her use yesterday to embrace her daughter? And the other day they were sticky and glistened with the harvest, one fleshy bean at a time.

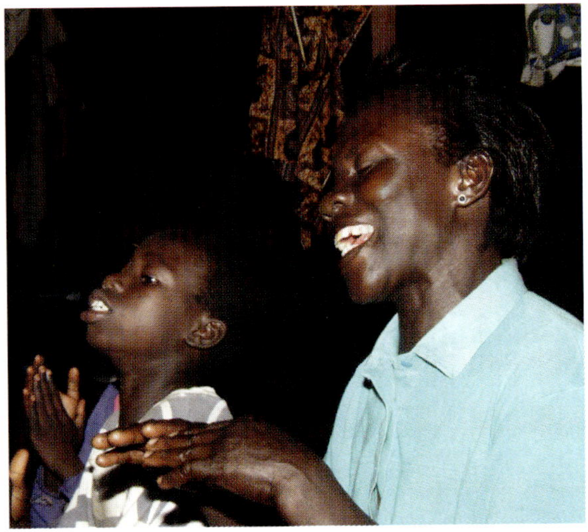

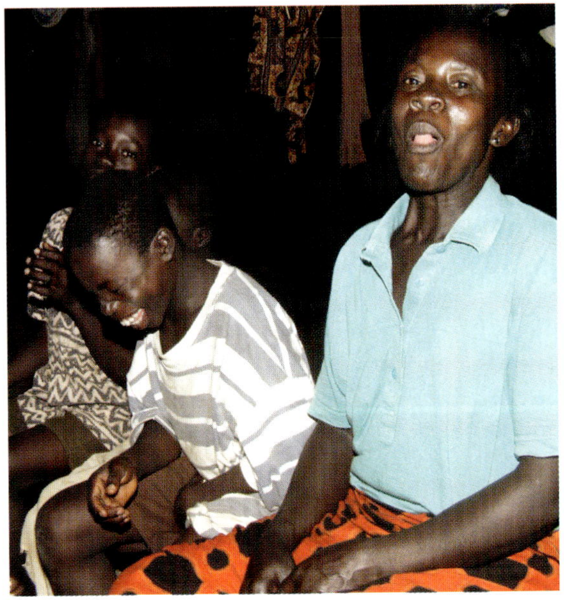

It was a musician from Ghana who excited me about African music and rhythm nearly 50 years ago. The gifted drummer made his music under the name of Guy Warren when he came to New York and turned on folks like Miles Davis and Thelonius Monk. I was in sixth grade when my mother gave me a Guy Warren record for Christmas. I've since worn out the record, but I still feel the rhythm. And I still know the first words I learned in another language which I picked up from Guy Warren off that recording, "*Shalom alekoum*". "Peace to you, my brother." I carried those words with me through the refugee camps of Sudan and the Shite Muslim region of northern India. I've carried my love for rhythm and African music to Odaho. So, blame it on Guy Warren, now known as Ghanaba or "son of Ghana", or on the full moon I just spotted coming up through the Onyina trees over Helena's cocoa—we're making our own music tonight at the Bempongs. Earlier in the week I taught Mary the Ghanaba chant I've carried all these years, "Aaaa-a-AH-ah", to which she replies (as she did through her cocoa trees the other day), "Aaaa-a-AH-ah." And now her boys are singing. "Aaaa-a-AH--ah.". And Paul Bempong thinks we're all a little "cocoa".

This afternoon Samson and I found two broken carpenter's block planes and part of a wooden rat trap laying in the road. We add pebbles to some partially crushed tin cans. Between rocks tapping on block planes and a rat trap along with the shaka-shaka-shaka of tin cans we have a pretty sweet rhythm section. And then add a nine-member chorus of "Aaaa-a-AH-ah"— we're smokin'. We might not be ready for a concert tour, but we can at least handle a recording studio, which I always carry in the front, left inside pocket of my shooting vest. Our music coming from that machine in the dirt sounds pretty hot. But it's more than hot for Veronica. She's never heard her singing voice before. She's blown away.

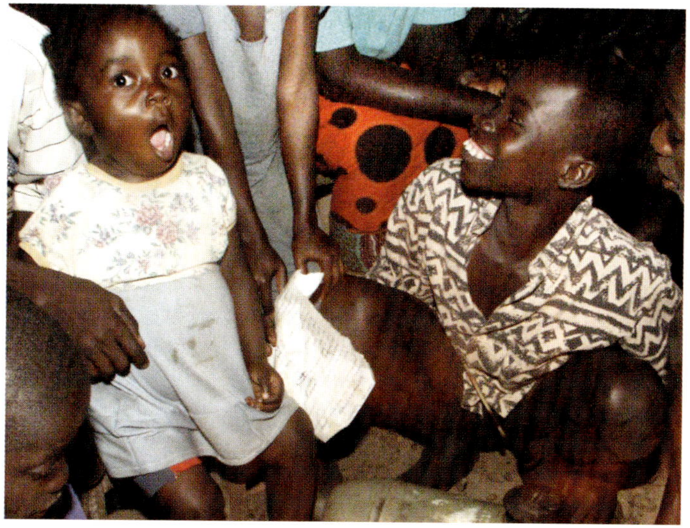

"Aaaa-a-AH-ah."

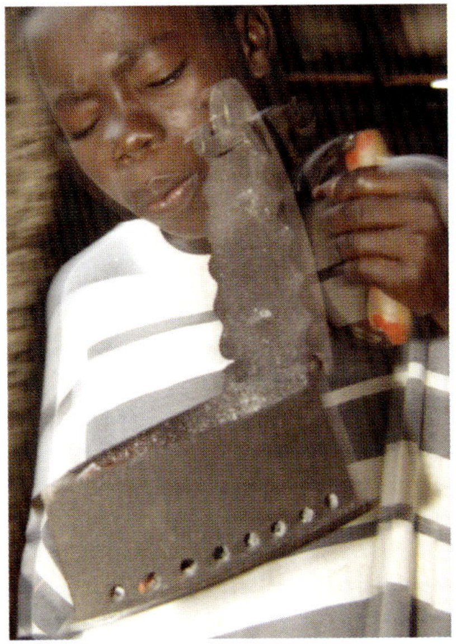

Mary's son, Samson, has recovered from the musical recording session last night and is back up at 5 fetching water at the nearby blowpipe for his mother. He and his brother Paul always seem to be helping their mother, either at home or on the farm. Samson spreads a cloth on a bench then walks over to the breakfast fire and picks up the cool end of a log. He walks back to the bench and opens the lid to a hand iron and knocks hot coals inside. He places his clean, brown shorts on the makeshift ironing board, and for the next ten minutes I watch this 13-year old boy iron his school uniform. He carefully irons the double pleats on his shorts, and periodically he stops to blow on the coals.

"Samson, why do you iron your clothes?," I ask Mary's son. He looks me straight in the eyes, has a pleasant smile and says, "Because it makes my clothes beautiful, and that makes me happy."

I leave Samson and pass the blowpipe where other school children are fetching water as sunrise starts to lift the morning fog. More cocoa comes by on the backs of strong, young men and I keep wandering the village.

Last night had its rhythm. Today's beat is felt in fetching water, ironing clothes, hauling cocoa—everything.

Children gather at the blowpipe to pump water for cooking, washing and drinking as sunrise pushes aside an early morning fog and Odaho wakes up to another day.

On past the blowpipe I come across a child preparing for school with a morning bath. His clean, pressed clothes are hanging on a nail nearby.

Up the path near my hibiscus I see a trickle of smoke coming from a small fire laid out among the surface root structure of a Kings of Way tree. A new neighbor friend is tending her small fire. Her name is Sara Brenya, and inside her tin can pot are three chunks of cassava cooking in some boiling water. She tells me in flawless English that her people believe "the leaves from Kings of Way tree relieve stomach distress." Her smile is medicine enough for me.

I cross paths with meandering sheep and a scattering of chickens, and then see the smoke from Appia and Mark's breakfast fire up ahead They also are doing their morning chores before school. As Appia grinds palm nuts, his younger brother Mark tends a pot of boiling water.

And one itinerant chicken darts through the kitchen making sure she stays clear of both boys and both pots . . .

Paul comes back with me tonight as he usually does to talk and watch me work by kerosene lamplight. We're both wondering what's happened to Emma who's been gone several days trying to get cash for the farmers—particularly Afua. He sent Kofi and some other helpers to her home, and they carried in the cocoa she had ready. I wanted to go with them, but unfortunately got my signals crossed, and missed getting pictures of them hauling in her cocoa.

I finish uploading the day's work into my laptop computer when Paul and I both yell as Emma storms in the room sounding a bit out of breath. "I got Afua's cocoa money. I could not deny that old woman," the Kuapa recorder practically shouts. "But I have to return to get money for the rest of the farmers."

Emma says he will pay the farmers what he can in the morning and set aside Afua's money. Hopefully she'll show up. He would then return to Kumasi and get the balance of the money and be back tomorrow night.

Emma double checks a farmer's record book and hands over the cash due while Felix Manu, Emma's assistant, helps the next farmer in line. Emma finishes making payments for the day and then heads back to Kuapa headquarters hoping the banks have freed up the money owed his farmers.

I don't understand the words, but Mary is honoring me with a farewell song. A relative has died in a village near Kumasi, and she leaves in a few minutes for the funeral. She knows I leave sometime tomorrow. This cocoa lady blesses me with the spirit in her song.

It was the music which first connected us months ago when she and her sons danced around her soap making fire. Her farewell song strengthens the bond.

The bond with Helena was sealed months ago in a clearing she and her son filled with new cocoa seedlings. The earth clung to her cutlass hand from hours of weeding, digging and planting under a hot, equatorial sun. When I recall how Gibran speaks of the "truth in the arms of the tillers of the soil", I think of her muddy hand. There is truth in the arms, but that hand covered in earth not only is grasping a cutlass, it's also holding hope. I've worked with farmers from here to Nicaragua to Thailand, Scotland, Maryland, India, the Philippines, Dominican Republic and Georgia. There is a universal truth I wrote years ago about all farmers, including Helena Bempong: "This land is sliced open and layered with seed and covered back over with the same measure of sweat, the same volume of hope, and watched and tended and scorned and loved in just the same way. Backs are broken in much the same manner on this land as back home—souls are toughened similarly, just as the faces leather under the same sun. . .and in the end there is common ground and home is the place where a man plants his plow, and all men plant to the same rhythm."

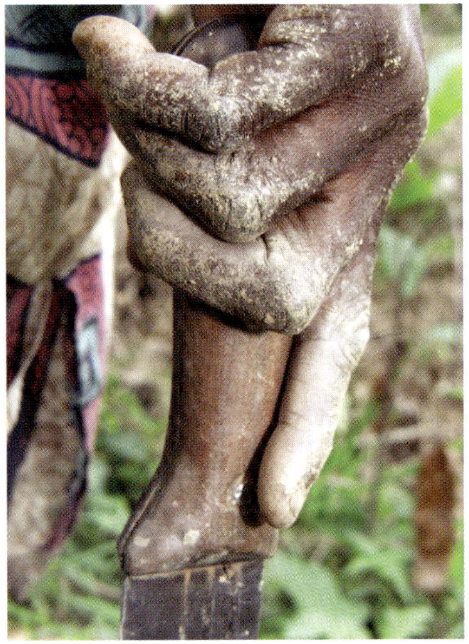

It is the rhythm of hope. That's what pulled me back to Africa—to see the fruition of hope plucked from trees, split open and shucked and hauled home on strong backs to dry. I also came back to see more of this cocoa farmer, her family and maybe discover the source of their hope.

It's right there covered with the good earth. Hope is in their hands.

Hope gives a cocoa farmer woman the strength to rise at 5 in the morning, see through the darkness and find the match to light one more breakfast fire for one more day. It pushes her up a beaten path, alongside cornfields and cocoa groves. It leads her to a hillside and gives her pause to pray and give thanks for the source of all hope. And just as she learned when she was a little girl, she grasps her digging staff with a muddy hand and makes room in the earth for another seedling—another harvest.

I came to this land four months ago in search of cocoa—the origin of chocolate. I'm leaving today with something not found on any list of ingredients on any bar of chocolate. It's there sewn up in each sack of dried cocoa, but it will never register on the most accurate of scales. I found hope in this village of cocoa farmers. The roots of hope run deep in this earth. All farmers know that truth.

The further civilization pulls itself away from the earth, the further it's removed from hope. The god of any religion never promises that darkness will not be part of life—only that the presence of darkness postulates the promise of light, of hope. As a photographer, I know that the light of a photograph is impossible without a period of darkness. I think that's what the poster in the Kuapa warehouse is all about. "Jesus Never Fails" these people because hope is always in their hands, in the good earth, and The Light is always near in spite of whatever darkness befalls them.

I'm getting ready to leave this village and see Anthony Bempong, Helena's husband, holding Veronica at the doorway. I don't understand what's being said, but I'm reminded again of hope as I watch this gentle cocoa farmer/school teacher speak

softly to his granddaughter. I think the concept of hope is passed from one generation to another. It's woven into their daily lives—unspoken— and strengthened by their closeness to the earth. They have accepted the truth that they can bury a tiny seedling in the ground, and five or six years later on that very spot there will be a mature cocoa tree full of ripe, golden cocoa pods. They also know that with a tremendous amount of work, the beans inside those pods can be dried, sold and turned into cash. The cash will buy whatever food they need to supplement what they cannot grow themselves. They know they can survive. It's in their hands. They also know they can take a little bit of that money and invest it in their cooperative, Kuapa Kokoo, which will treat them fairly, pay them for their effort and even give them back a little more. In some ways it's not much more than they received

for their effort years ago, before Kuapa. But I think I just witnessed an example of how this organization has made a difference.

Although Afua never made the one-hour walk to get her cocoa money, Emma walked to her. Paul and I went with him. We were like a bunch of kids laughing and joking—even singing "Blessed Assurance" in something like two-and-a-half part harmony walking through the cocoa. "This is my story, this is my song. . ."

That was nearly four hours ago. I'm on my way to the airport in Accra. Helena is riding with me as far as Kumasi. Our taxi crosses the last bridge to Odaho, and I think how lost I was four months ago crossing this same bridge for the first time, going the other way. I look downstream and can still picture Emma only moments ago leaving Afua. He bends over and cups his right hand to cool off with a splash of water from this same river. His money satchel is a bit lighter, but it's full of hope.

Epilogue

. . . So many trails run through this manuscript, it's difficult finding a way home. The 6,000 miles between my studio in the woods—where winter is cold and white and more than a foot deep—and Odaho is almost unimaginable. But I try. First I must take Afua's hands to lead me back.

I light a smudge stick of dried sage and place it near a photograph of her hands on my writing desk at the window. The desk is made from a three-inch by five foot slab of redwood burl—a close cousin to Onyina, and the color of dried cocoa—the color of Afua's hands. Sage is not the smoke of a breakfast fire, but it's very close and comforting. I crack the top window, and the smoke is drawn outside, on through the woods of tulip poplars and oaks and by now is drifting across the black ribbon of river slicing through this snow-filled gorge. It's moving on up the distant hillside, skimming the ridge line and by now is far off to the east—somewhere between here and a cocoa grove an hour west of Odaho. Now my mind catches up with Paul, Emma and Afua . . .

The old woman moves quickly though the forest, then darts along a massive, downed Onyina tree which serves as a bridge across the river. My first thought is this tiny old woman has turned into a lizard scampering over this very big log. (But months later, when I enlarge and study the only photograph I was able to get of her on the tree, I immediately see the "tiny" lady has grown. It's there in this slice of time. The massive Onyinaa tree and the strands of well-defined muscles running up her right arm are part of each other. Her arm looks like a miniature of this 15-foot tree trunk.) We catch up with Afua at the edge of her settlement where more cocoa is drying on her racks. I'm not sure what she's saying to Emma, but she puts down her gathering basket with cutlass and jug of water, then goes inside her home. In a few minutes she appears in a clean, white muslin dress. She pulls a stool over for Emma, and the two of them sit in the shade to conduct their business. Emma opens his black satchel and pulls out a stack of cedis, the Ghanaian currency. He pays Afua the money he's been trying to get to her for days. The Kuapa recorder said, "I could not deny that old woman." And he hasn't.

Afua pauses and glances at the money. She gets up and goes inside. When she comes out she's no longer holding the cash, but she hands Emma a small box. She says something to him, and he opens the lid and pulls out an empty bottle of medicine. She smiles and speaks again to Emma who translates, "She says now she can buy her own medicine."

Hope carves trails in an old woman's hands
then plows furrows up her arms,
and all paths lead back home
where food is never scarce
and the medicine is always half full.

Hope sometimes moves on bamboo wheels and rides on discarded timbers. It digs its feet into the ground and moves on because it knows it can.

Hope is the color of sun-dried cocoa and smells of a place where "Jesus Never Fails". It wraps itself around a digging staff and plunges itself into the ground—pries itself back, then gently lies down in the cool earth and covers each new seedling and each green leaf with the promise of a good harvest yet to come.

Hope thrusts itself into a cocoa tree and knows exactly where to slice each stem of golden pod. It slashes and rips and shucks each pod. It drops into one more gathering basket filling up thoughts of a kinder September when food becomes more precious.

Hope rides the backs of cocoa men with heavy loads of chocolate in the rough, then catches the rhythm and stirs each bean drying in the sun.

Hope rises at 4:30 in the morning to build a fire for breakfast. It fetches the water and scrubs the pots, and irons crisp, hot pleats into a pair of school shorts—just because hope is beautiful and can make a boy dream.

Hope picks pretty red tomatoes and carries them off to market. It sings soft songs to an infant who may never know the taste of chocolate, but will always taste the sweetness of hope.

This hope is the hope for all, and cannot be denied—not one old cocoa farmer woman, nor 40,000 more.

Hope is an angel standing watch over this land like a majestic Onyina tree at sundown. Its roots weave themselves through every inch of this land—every aspect of this life. Its wings cast shadows of light spreading across this village and a thousand thousand villages throughout the Developing World.

Hope
brings its own sweet rain
at just the right time,
turning plump and golden
day after day,
because
hope is a fruit
always in season,
brought home on
sweat-soaked backs
and left to dry
for one more harvest—
a harvest of hope.

Divine
WITH A HEART
Rodoxin
1000